The Old Lady Book

A Book of Instruction and Enlightenment for the Formerly Young

I0176884

by

Diana Hannon Forrester

Cover art by Amanda Morley

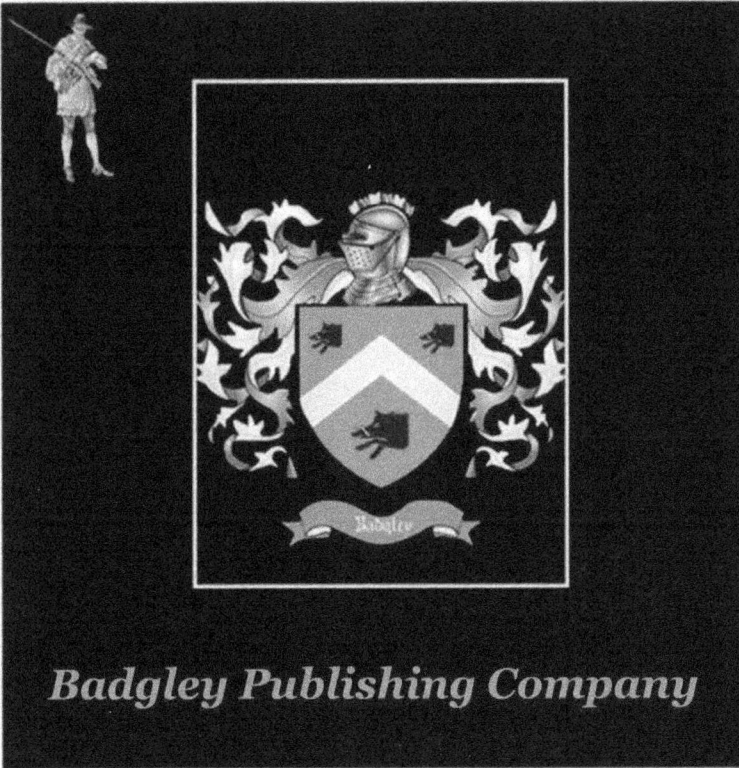

Badgley Publishing Company

ISBN 978-0-9988045-3-8

This book is dedicated to the memory of

Ruth Banerito

She lived to the age of 97. She was a chemist at the U.S. Department of Agriculture who helped perfect Permanent-Press Fabric. We all love you Ruth.

INTRODUCTION

IN THE BEGINNING

ADULTS R US

THE SCARY STUFF

THE REALLY SCARY STUFF

Introduction

There are instruction books about everything: how to win friends and influence people; how to raise a healthy child; how to be a good wife; how to make a million dollars and hundreds more. I'm going to try leading us formerly young women through the maze of old-lady-hood. If we are female; if we don't die young; we will get to be old ladies with no effort. The passage of time will take care of the details.

By the time we start to "feel" old we will have had some peak moments. Maybe we've gotten married, had children, or made partner in the firm. We can do it all these days, or so the story goes. We will also have suffered some losses. One thing we old ladies have in common is we have survived. Whatever has happened so far, we have lived through it. Maybe not with a lot of grace and maybe not with much desire to go on. But we must vow to go on as long as we can and then do it. Who knows what the payoff will be.

There are stages to go through. There is growth and getting through childhood. Marriage and the birth and raising of our own children. Our children leave home and we are alone with whomever our spouse has become. We strive to survive as whomever we have become. It's a roller coaster and mostly it is fun.

Then comes a day when we are alone. Left to face whatever lies ahead. Some of it is scary; some of it is painful; some of it just has to be gotten through and all of this is true. I have been there and I know.

I'm sending you stories of things that have happened and things that might have happened as I teetered my way to old ladyhood. I hope you enjoy the stories and they help you remember some stories of your own. I hope they make you smile and bask in the time you are an old lady. Long may it last.

When I was in high school I went steady with a boy who could dance. We were poetry in motion in the school gym whether we were doing the stroll, or the pony, or the jitterbug. We were absolutely heavenly on the slow dances gliding across the floor like we were on wheels. I can still feel his arms around me light as feathers. I wore his class ring with great gobs of angora wrapped around the finger hole so it would fit. We all did. We'd wait in the back hall of the school for the guys to clean up from whatever game they had been playing. They came to collect us and then we'd dance. It was wonderful. Their damp skin and the heavenly fragrance of after shave. Play the music; let your body move to the rhythm; close your eyes and imagine the past. You can time-travel in your own mind.

For me it's the dancing. For you it may be something else. The sound of rain on the roof, the sound of your dad's whistle telling you it's time to come in for the night. It could be anything that takes you back to those innocent times. Reclaim them for yourself and enjoy them all over again.

Old ladies can be a rowdy bunch. I knew a lot of them when I ran the program for seniors in my town. We all got together once a month to assemble a newsletter. I was thirty-four and still on the outside looking in. It was a revelation to me.

They laughed and talked about their lives, their husbands, their children. We had a bronze medalist from a long-past Olympics, we had the mother of the woman who designed the "Coke" can, we had a woman who cooked for the jail on the rare occasion there was a prisoner. They speculated about other old ladies they knew who had men living with them. "Those were the days," one said. "We'd pull down the blinds and rip off a piece." It was my first view of what lay ahead.

I don't know everything about being an old lady, but I know some things. I know I'm still having fun. We do lose some functions as we pass through the forties, fifties, sixties, seventies and eighties. Perfect eyesight goes quietly. We may not even know it's gone until we're fitted with glasses. Teeth (in my case) went early. I can take them out and store them in the cupboard. Our knees may hurt, we may need a cane. We can't run fast and jumping rope gets more challenging. We get a new appreciation for, "It's always something". It truly is always something.

Whatever our age we need to get out of bed to see what is going to happen today and we need to keep smiling as long as we can. Come along with me and see for yourself what it means to be an old lady.

Diana Hannon Forrester
2018

How it happened to me

It was a wonderful soft Ohio evening
Summer time.
The fragrance of my roses floated on the air.
Children were playing wiffle ball on the cul-de-sac where I
live.
I was sitting on my porch, sipping my evening martini and
enjoying,
Feeling fine.
One of the older girls (about twelve, I think) walloped the
ball.
All the outfielders missed their play
And the ball came bouncing my way.
I smiled warmly as one of the outfielder girls ran toward me.
She turned her head and yelled to the rest of the kids,
"Don't hit the old lady! Don't hit the old lady!"
I was puzzled.
Old Lady?
I didn't see any old lady.
I looked over my shoulder.
Sure enough, there was nobody there!

"Like I say, it just creeps up on you.
One day you're young
and the next day your bosoms sag
and your chin drops,
and you're wearing a rubber girdle.
But you don't know you're old."

Fannie Flagg
Fried Green Tomatoes

It's All Relative

"Age, like beauty, is in the eye of the beholder"

My grandmother was an old lady when I met her...fifty-two. She was a big, tall woman, strong as an ox in my eyes. She attended school till fourth grade when she was "let-out" to wealthy neighbors where she helped cook and clean the house.

She was married at the age of twenty-four to a man she had never met. He traveled from Indiana to Illinois where they were married before returning home to their life together. Aside from being a good wife, she was to be mother to the two children her new husband had to raise after the death of his first wife.

I learned much later she was pregnant as a bride and surely hadn't much choice in the matter of the marriage. My grandmother could wring a chicken's neck with one flick of her wrist and send the chicken running around the yard with its head flopping every which way, then dunk it in boiling water and pluck off its feathers.

She put up canned goods for a family of seven (she and my grandfather had three more children). She worked hard: mid-wifed babies, did laundry, gardened, baked bread, cleaned wallpaper. Seems there wasn't a thing she couldn't do.

I always knew my grandmother was old. From my earliest memory she wore glasses and could take her teeth in and out. She played canasta with her friends at her kitchen table and drank coffee with them at the neighborhood diner. They were loud and they laughed a lot. Eventually they taught me to play in case they needed a fourth.

My grandmother was old all my life.

Mrs. Twible, my first-grade teacher, was old. She was married but had no children yet. She had charge of me seven hours a day. I had to respect her and do what she told me. She taught me how to read and write. (thank you Mrs. Twible) I've enjoyed this for over a half century. Looking back, I'd guess she was all of twenty-five and time was on her side in every way that mattered.

My friends and I, in the anonymity of the playground or the cloak room (yes, we still had cloak rooms back then) or especially the rowdy boys in class, might refer to her as "Old Lady Twible".

The other first grade teacher was Mrs. Parvas. She had gray hair and was also first grade teacher to my father back in the day. Any fool could figure out she was an old lady.

I have a friend who is an old lady. I am sure of it, but I called her one day to get her scoop on this.

"I'm seventy-two," I told her. "I've decided that qualifies me as an old lady."

"You're wrong," she said. "I think you have to be eighty, maybe eighty-five to meet the requirements for old lady-hood."

I was taken aback. I knew for a fact she could out walk me. She could out-think me and she had better manners than I would ever have. She'd had her night driving privileges revoked by the Bureau of Motor Vehicles two years ago. When the sun went down, so did she.

She'd been a canteen girl, moving to Florida at the height of World War II to help entertain the GIs there. She considered it her patriotic duty.

She coaxed the men she met to take her to Italian restaurants and judged their social status on how they handled the task of eating spaghetti.

She worked before it was the feminist Betty Friedan, Gloria Steinem thing to do. She was happy with a job as an executive secretary at the same time that Sandra Day O'Conner, despite her law degree, could only get a job as a secretary in a law firm. My friend lived with discrimination, but she was happy with her job. Eventually she went to college and became a teacher. She retired from that job after twenty fruitful years.

She is ninety-four years old. I attended her ninetieth birthday party. It was a fine affair. She was perfectly gracious to the (mostly) other old ladies who came to help her celebrate.

One thing I know for sure: who among us is an old lady is strictly a matter of our point of view. It has nothing to do with our actual age.

In the Beginning

"Reaching old age begins at birth."

Diana Forrester

The Violet Hour

Laura Cramer's belly was swollen with her first child, due to be born in a matter of weeks. Her back ached from her pregnant posture. Her feet hurt from walking the fields looking for Carmen, the cow who had a baby of her own that day. Laura found her three miles from the house, down by the stream. She looked very proud of herself. Together they led the calf home on wobbly legs. Laura smiled a soft smile remembering. She removed her apron and laid it on one of the two straight backed chairs at the kitchen table. She placed palms near her spine and stretched backwards to work her compressed vertebrae. It felt good.

John had gone to the barn for a final check on the livestock. He was a hard worker and overly cautious since Buss Keeton's milk cow was accidently left out overnight and eaten by a small pack of wolves that had been frequenting the area.

Laura gathered up a kimono she was embroidering for the baby and went to the porch. She sat in the swing and leaned back, relaxing finally after her long day. Gratitude filled her heart for the wonderful home she and John were building. The baby rolled inside her and she lay a calming hand on him. At least she hoped it was a him. Laura wanted sons...tall, handsome, good sons like their father.

From the porch Laura could look out over the thick loamy soil. It stretched for miles and in the distance, she imagined she could see the Johnson's house four miles away. She could really see the thirty acres of corn John had planted last week.

The plants had already become a little green fuzz on the soil. They were darkened by the twilight but in the morning, they would be green again. She could also see the small plot closer to the house where she would plant her truck patch after the baby was born. Laura felt safe, she felt strong, she believed life was good.

She could hear John's boots crunching on the path to the house. She heard him kick the barn dirt loose from them before he got close to the porch. Laura started her needle flowing and was bent to her sewing when John turned the corner to the house.

"Everything secure in the barn?" she asked.

"Tight as a ragtime drum," he said. He walked behind the swing and lifted Laura's hair off her back. He kissed her neck where the curls were short and persistent...where the dampness of the day's work lingered. His lips were scratchy from being dried by the sun.

"Sit?" Laura said, patting the swing beside her. John walked around and sat beside her. He smelled of sweat and dirt and rope and motor oil. They had saved to buy a tractor which John said would make all the difference. "We can plant more than we need," he told her. "Half for ourselves and half to take to market. In five years it will make us comfortable."

That had been two years ago, and John had been right. They had a nice nest egg stashed away. Half of it was in the bank and half of it was buried in a metal box out behind the well.

John sat beside his wife and she laid her embroidery in her lap. He took her hand and kissed each finger. "I love you," he said.

"I love you, too, Laura said. "And our son." John rubbed the mound of her belly and held his hand firmly to feel the baby kick.

"He's kicking up a storm," John said. "Rarin' to get into the world and get going."

Laura sighed, lay her head on her husband's shoulder and looked out into the violet dusk.

*"Childhood is a perilous time
but most of us survive."*

Diana Forrester

Children of My Own

My early memories are shadowy and small. Walking off to Sunday School when I was only four. Crossing Indiana Route 67 where three black cocker pups were killed by speeding cars, but I was spared. Perhaps my mother hung out the front door and watched me to safety. Perhaps my father took me by the hand and crossed me over, but I fared better than the dogs. From there the path to town was straight and paved and watched over by houses sitting on a hill.

I believe my heels clicked like a tap dancer's with the seriousness of my mission and if my parents worried, I never saw it. I'd return from church and they were still thick with sleep, crusty eyed and young, perhaps still growing as they were only twenty-three.

I had no life of my own and lived or died at their whim. We were all in a fragile little boat and they guided it as best they could.

My first memories that were purely my own came in second grade. The Frazee twins talking about their dancing lessons and their tutus and everything I could imagine a girl might want. They were cookie cutter girls with short dark hair that never poked about unruly and who surely had names of their own, though I can't retrieve them now. They had little plastic purses with combs, bobby pins and embroidered hankies their mother washed and ironed. And that same year Charlie Watts sang *Darktown Strutters Ball* on the stage in the park one soft summer night. He wore patent leather shoes that glittered in the lights, pants creased to a razor's edge and a stiff white shirt with pleats across the front. He was prettier than I would ever be.

I yearned to be like them. My life has been filled with yearning and maybe it started there in second grade with the Frazee twins and Charlie Simms or maybe it started sooner, when all I did was walk to church alone.

My father started college when I was nine. He had a wife, my brother, me and a mangy mixed-breed dog who wiggled and smiled and ate what was left when dinner was done. We lived for a while in a green trailer home where the ice man still came with huge blocks to last the week and puddle on the floor. I wore sturdy brown shoes and dresses handed down from my cousin who was two years older and whose father sold insurance and didn't go to college. We moved a lot and the butcher gave my father bones which my mother made into soup or stew.

My father had an old gray Buick that hated starting in the cold. I'd hear the metallic UNNA-UNNA-UNNA of the car failing to start and the hot, black cursing of my father that almost always seemed to get the car to spark and go. We lived at the bottom of a hill that the school bus couldn't negotiate in the snow, so I missed a lot of school that winter and watched television on the day that Elizabeth became queen.

Summer nights I could lay in my bed and hear the laughter and the music from a dance pavilion across the lake. It seems to me now that I could hear the clink of glasses and the swishing of the women's skirts as they danced into the night.

I'm not sure what is true, but I formed dreams on that lake. I was only ten years old when I did it and I'm not sure that is old enough to be trusted with hopes and dreams that will last a life time.

My father graduated college then and took my mother to his prom in a strapless dress of American beauty rose with yards of netting in the skirt. She was the most beautiful thing I had ever seen, and I believe the image of beauty I carried with me through my life.

I was eighteen soon and a college girl myself. I lived upstairs over a door with a green wooden screen that cracked like a baseball bat when it fell shut. I wore silken things that swirled around my legs. They were soft and erotic to the touch. I was full of myself and fertile then. A Botticelli's girl, though Twiggy was in fashion.

It was men by then, always men and dreams trying to come true. Down the hall was an older man who took arty pictures of common things. One day he met me in the hall and asked to borrow my skirt. I took it off and sat on a hard chair in my underwear while he arranged it just so and placed wilted flowers from a fetid vase around it. His pants bulged while he worked, and he cast crafty glances my way.

I kept my face stern, unyielding but later I laughed with a lover who reached all the hidden places in me. A man not meant for marriage but who loved me well and sharply while he lasted. We were arrogantly young and cruel. I was on the pill and always wet between my legs. Those were the days my friend. I thought they'd never end.

Then came love that was meant to end my yearning, to fulfill my dreams, with a boy/man who was needy in areas where I was rich. I wanted to love him whole, to have his children and to change the world...futile acts and dreams formed by a ten-year-old. It was doomed from the start, but I was too certain of myself to see. The babies came one, two, three and elders smiled and shook their heads, "Do you know what's causing this?"

It was a golden time, filled with the promise of youth and the glory of dreams coming true. Life was baby poop and yeasty bread and things popping from the soil.

I was mother earth with children of my own and a man to wrap my life around till he found another girl.

I cried, I raged, I could not be a graceful loser, hard as I might try. But I was strong and still ready to march off alone like I had done at four, waiting for nobody, needing nobody, yearning still.

On Eating Our Children

*"I have been assured by a very knowing
American, of my acquaintance in London,
that a young healthy child, well-nursed,
is at a year, most delicious, nourishing and
wholesome food whether stewed,
roasted, baked or broiled
and I have no doubt that it will equally
serve in a fricassee or ragout."*

Jonathon Swift
A Modest Proposal

Growing Up

*"We may look old and wise
to the outside world
but to each other,
we're still in seventh grade."*

Charlotte Gray

The Pit

I was eager to grow up, eager to become a woman and understand the meaning of life. I was twelve the summer that it happened and when it did, I only wanted to go back to being a child, innocent of responsibility and consequences. By then it was too late.

"The rattlers have hatched," my father said. "Charlie Watts says the pit looks like purgatory when they come out to sun themselves." His brow scrunched together like they did sometimes when he was real serious.

I chewed my toast and watched my mother stirring scrambled eggs, her shoulders hunched in a blue plaid robe. My father called her Anne Boleyn when she got like this, missing England, where he'd found and courted her during the War. I'd heard the story often enough to know it by heart. My mother always cried when she got to the part about leaving England. Nothing got her over it but my brother Danny who was six that year. She said she could see the English sky in his eyes and he made her smile.

"Julia, you stay away from that Pit," my father said. "We'll start shooting the snakes on Saturday."

My mother shuffled to the table and spooned eggs onto our plates. They weren't cooked dry, and I could feel my stomach tighten as a narrow, milky river formed around the pile of shiny eggs.

"Eat Julia," my father said. I closed my eyes, begged God to keep my throat from pinching shut and forked eggs into my mouth. I could feel my father's eyes on me, but I didn't look at him.

He stood, ruffled Danny's hair and kissed my mother good-bye. "Help your mother today, Julia," he said to me before he left.

My mother rinsed her coffee cup, set it in the sink. "Look after Danny," she said. "I'm going back to bed." It was our secret. I knew not to tell my father when she was depressed and slept all day and I was Danny's caretaker. Danny went to his room and I began clearing the table and stacking dishes in the sink.

My parents called it a passion pit. Mom clucked her tongue against her teeth and crunched her eyebrows together and Dad's eyes twinkled when he talked about it. It was really a gravel pit dug into the side of hills that bordered the summer lake where we lived year-round because it was cheap, and my dad was studying engineering on the GI Bill. A one lane path let into the pit and the sides soared and widened like a funnel to the sky. A few boulders jutted from the floor, still half buried and too huge to dig out. It drew kids like a magnet.

Stevie Sims and I visited whenever we could, looking for treasures and adventure. The walls were unreliable and small avalanches of sand and gravel sluiced and pinged constantly making the hair on our necks tingle with the delicious fear of children. We heard bits of stories about children buried alive and teenagers drinking, dancing and singing and the sheriff being called. The adult's faces would go blank and the subject would change when we entered the room. This made us more resolute.

We carried in Twinkies and bottles of soda pop, sat cross legged on the canyon floor and talked about what was important to us that summer: the New York Yankees, Elizabeth the new queen, sixth grade and what it all meant. We found crispy snake skins, brittle rattles, scratchy to the hand and exciting to hold, but we never saw the snakes. The Pit always made me feel on the edge of something important, but I wasn't sure what it was.

Sometimes we found tire tracks and empty beer cans and once we found a brassiere, white as snow against the dark gravel floor. It had an edge of narrow lace and a thin layer of foam rubber padding. I giggled over it and Stevie blushed red when I slipped the straps over my shoulders and paraded for him. We hid it under a rock before we left and when we returned, it was gone, hidden by the shifting walls.

When I had wiped the table clean and had the dishes soaking in hot, soapy water, I hurried out the door, closing it carefully so it wouldn't bang in its wooden frame and disturb my mother. I ran down the road to the Sim's cottage. Stevie's mother was singing inside. I pulled open the wooden screen door, stepped inside and let it bang shut behind me.

"Morning, Julia," Mrs. Sims said. She wore yellow pedal pushers and a flowered blouse. Her hair was pulled back into a pony tail that bounced as she moved about her kitchen. "Stevie's gone down to uncover the boat," she said. "I'm going fishing this morning. Maybe catch our supper." She winked one sparkling brown eye at me. "You want a waffle? Or some juice?"

"No thanks, Mrs. Sims. I ate already. I'll just go down and help Stevie with the boat."

"Hey Julia," he said. "You want to go fishing?"

I grabbed an end of the boat cover and helped him fold. "No," I said. "We've got to get to the Pit and look at the rattlers. My dad says they're thick."

"Do you think we should?" he said. "Rattlers can be dangerous."

"I think I will die if I don't see them," I said. They're going to kill them Saturday. We have to go today."

Stevie nodded, grinned and stowed the boat cover under the rear seat of the boat. He moved the tackle box and several poles into the boat. Then he cupped his hands around his mouth and shouted toward the house. "Mom, the boat's ready."

Mrs. Sims came out the front door, a plaid insulated bag dangling from her hand. "You kids want to go?" she called. Stevie and I exchanged glances, shook our heads. Mrs. Sims went off alone. We stood on the dock and watched while she maneuvered the boat out into the lake, steering with one hand, waving with the other.

We watched her out of sight, then ran into the house, put sandwiches, sodas and cookies into a bag and slammed out the back door towards the road. Danny was sitting on the steps.

"I have to watch him," I said to Stevie. I shrugged. "My mom's sleeping."

Danny tagged behind us kicking gravel as we set off down the road toward the Pit. The cottages all faced the lake, so we passed only garages and back yards as we made our way.

"Did you see the picture of Elizabeth in her crown in the morning paper?" I asked. "She's so beautiful."

"Philip should be king," Steve said. " Queens can't lead soldiers."

"They can so," I said.

"Philip has the sword."

"You don't need a sword to lead soldiers," I said. "You need a brain." Danny ran ahead, excited to be included in our adventure.

"The Yankees are going to take the series for sure this year," Stevie said. "I bet they get it in four games flat."

"Ha," I said. "You can never count the Dodgers out till the last ball is thrown." We chatted easily as we walked. I kept an eye on Danny and the excitement of seeing the rattlers grew underneath it all.

The road dead-ended into a hill covered with trees, sticker bushes heavy with berries and the outcroppings of boulders. We looked all around to be sure no one was looking before we darted into the narrow path.

The Pit had the echoey silence of a church. A quiet that was huge and made me feel insignificant. We three stood silently, respecting the place. Danny took my hand. His was small, dry and a little bit gritty. I held it while we scanned the walls for signs of life. A narrow blade of sunlight cut the far wall near the top, but there was no sign of rattlers.

"They come out for the sun," I said. "We'll have to wait." I peered at the line of light on the walls. It wouldn't be long.

Stevie dropped the vinyl bag to the ground and unzipped it. "Let's have a drink before the soda gets hot." He lifted three bottles out of the bag and popped the caps off with an opener that was hooked to the zipper by a string.

Danny gathered the metal caps and sailed them into the dark wall. Gravel pinged and fell. The sound bounced back at us.

Stevie dropped to a sitting position and turned his face to the sky as he drained the soda from the bottle. He wiped his mouth with the back of his hand and burped. "You see any snakes?" he asked.

"Nope, but I know they are here." I sipped my soda.

"I'd like to be queen," I said. "And ride around in a carriage with footmen and tell everybody what to do."

"You're nuts," Stevie said. "Queens and kings never get to be just regular and go to work in the morning or go fishing in their own boat. They have subjects to look after and when things go wrong they have to be responsible for everything. Besides, my mom said it would be like living in a fish bowl. I'd rather be a ball player."

"I'd like it. Danny'd get to be a prince and my mother would laugh. We'd have to move to England."

Stevie stretched out and propped his head on his hand. His eyes searched the sides of the Pit. I looked up and the band of sunlight reached halfway down the wall. Soon it would reach the spot where Stevie and I were sitting. We'd see the rattlers. A tingle of excitement ran up my spine.

"Do you think we'll see them first, or hear them first?"

"I don't think they'll come out while we're here," *Stevie* said.

Danny was working his way around the edge of the gravel pit, getting close to the sunny side. "Watch out for rattlers," I yelled at him. He zinged one of the pop bottle lids toward us. It pinged and skipped like a flat stone on water. Danny laughed and disappeared behind a boulder set close to the wall. Stevie and I watched for him to run out the other side. Instead we saw his pop bottle loop up and hit the wall above the boulder. It raised a mushroom of dust that looked like a bomb and the wall began to fall away. Danny's scream was high pitched and short.

There was nothing we could do. Danny was gone by the time we ran to the spot. . . trapped by the boulder and buried by a ton of sand that still slid and tumbled from the top of the wall. We tried digging him out, but more gravel fell over our hands than we were able to move. It tumbled down and puddled at our feet until they were buried, too, and we had to jump back out of the way ourselves.

Stevie and I stood looking at one another till the gravely tinkling stopped and silence returned. We were helpless. We knew Danny was already dead. There was no hurry to get home, no hurry to grow up, no way to escape what had happened.

Stevie took my hand and pulled me away. "Come on," he said. "We'd better get some help." I nodded and we gathered up our pop bottles, silently stowed them in the vinyl bag and began the long walk home, leaving Danny with the rattlers.

Children

So, we were young, and we built our lives, often around the children we created or the vocations we chose. I know you remember that. So do I.

I learned that God, in his wisdom, gave me four children because he knew I would drive a lesser number crazy.

The days were long and the years were short.

Now I wonder where they've gone. What happened to the children who believed I knew how to solve every problem. Those children who believed I would be there to feed them breakfast after a peaceful night of rest. The same children who when they reached fourteen thought I knew nothing and never would. Oh, life is fun, and it is interesting.

Some of us wanted to live long enough to become a problem to our children. I have to tell you secretly that I love it. It is a hidden reward for allowing them to live the many times they deserved severe and perhaps fatal retribution. The times they were late getting home and forgot to call. The times they forgot to tell me it was my turn to bake cupcakes for the Halloween Party; the times they swore they were spending the night at a friend's house.

I recently had a meeting scheduled at my house. I forgot about it and went to supper with other friends. The meeting friends got in touch with my daughter who came to search my house with fear and trepidation, hoping not to stumble over my cold, dead body. It could happen, I admit, but when she told me about it in a scolding tone, all I could do was laugh.

As a parent, I learned that no news was good news. If my children were missing (or late) and the police, the hospital, or a good close friend didn't call, everything would be fine. How many nights did I sit up waiting for one of my children to creep quietly into the house? Who knows? Who cares? I had to learn to measure good times by the fact that "nobody died, and nobody was pregnant". I had learned that no news was good news and it's time they learned it, too.

I have reached the age where my survival is not assured. I can no longer be reasonably expected to turn up after dropping out of sight temporarily. I could be lying dead in my bed. But in the meantime . . . I get to be a problem.

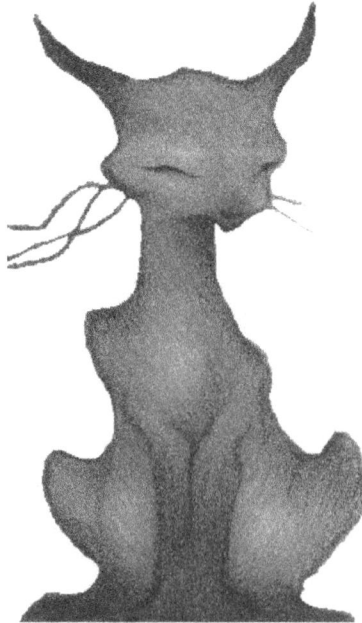

Things I've Learned from My Children

1. A king size water bed holds enough water to fill a 2000 square foot room four inches deep.

2. If you spray hair spray on dust bunnies and run over them with roller blades, they will ignite.

3. A 3-year-olds voice is louder than 200 adults in a crowded restaurant.

4. If you hook a dog leash over a ceiling fan, the motor is not strong enough to rotate a 42-pound boy wearing Batman underwear and a superman cape.

5. It is strong enough, however, if tied to a paint can, to spread paint on all four walls of a 20 by 20 room.

6. You should not throw baseballs up when the ceiling fan is on. A ceiling fan can hit a baseball a long way.

7. The glass in windows (even double pane) doesn't stop a baseball hit by a ceiling fan.

8. When you hear the toilet flush and the words "Uh-oh," it's already too late.

9. Brake fluid mixed with Clorox makes smoke and lots of it.

10. A six-year-old can start a fire with a flint rock even though a 36-year-old man says they can only do it in the movies.

11. Certain Legos will pass through the digestive tract of a four-year-old.

Play dough and microwave should never be used in the same sentence.

12. Super glue is forever.

13. No matter how much Jell-O you put in a swimming pool, you still can't walk on water.

14. Pool filters do not like Jell-O.

15. VCR's do not eject PB&J sandwiches even though TV commercials show they do.

16. Garbage bags do not make good parachutes.

17. Marbles in gas tanks make lots of noise.

18. You probably do not want to know what that odor is.

19. Always look in the oven before you turn it on. Plastic toys do not like ovens.

20. The fire department in Austin, TX has a 5-minute response time.

21. The spin cycle on the washing machine does not make earthworms dizzy.

22. It will, however, make cats dizzy.

23. Cats throw up twice their body weight when dizzy.

24. The mind of a six-year-old is wonderful.

Anonymous mother (has to be a mom) from Austin, TX

Lady in Waiting

There is a picture of me somewhere. In it I am not quite two. My shoes are remarkably scuffed considering the length of my legs and the limited amount of freedom I have to go where I might. My toes are balanced ballerina-like on the cement steps at my grandmother's house. The house and my grandmother are both long gone. My fingers are small and they are pointed one toward the other with the simple elegance of childhood. There is a look of consternation and anticipation on my little face; a question is knit into the wrinkles of my brow. I am clearly waiting, waiting for something or someone.

My soul and a good part of my life are captured in that picture. It is almost like a magic looking glass that saw far into the future. When the picture was taken I was perhaps waiting to walk to town for ice cream or waiting for my nap or maybe waiting for my father to come home from World War II.

As time passed, the list of things I waited for grew longer. There was waiting for my brother to be born, waiting for school to start, waiting for the bus to come, waiting for summer, waiting for Christmas, waiting to grow taller, waiting to lose my baby fat, waiting for high school, waiting for my first kiss, waiting to graduate, waiting for college to start, waiting for the right man to come along, waiting for the other shoe to drop.

And the milestones were passed and another phase of waiting ended. But I never quite finished, quite in-the-know as I thought I should be. I never felt the event and the waiting had been quite worthwhile. Perhaps the significance of each event was hidden in the shadow of its achievement. I'm not quite sure but the selfish confidence of youth gave way to something else. Something I couldn't name.

I was waiting to catch on to what the rest of the world knew that had so obviously escaped me. Waiting to feel like the grown up I'd sometimes appear to be. Waiting to be let in on whatever cosmic joke God was playing on us all. I was sure there was a punch line I had missed. I waited for it, searched and waited for understanding and direction. I thought it might come the same way the Miss America crown came. With the swell of musical chords, the emotional voice of Bert Park singing and an audience cheering because the moment had arrived.

There was waiting for the wedding, waiting for the babies to be born while my body incubated and my life went on hold. I learned to live around the corners of the lives of my husband and my children. I learned to wait my turn. What really mattered was my husband's job and furthering his education. That and my children's potential, what was good for them, their bottles and their diapers.

In the middle of the night there was waiting with my eyes wide open for them to wake crying hungrily, there was waiting for their first words and steps, and their first days of school. There was waiting for my husband to come home. It was a circle, I could see. I waited for it to end.

I did it because the waiting was full of wonder and possibilities. I got to be important to my children and serve a purpose in the world. To them I was tall, I knew everything. I was strong and smart with answers to their questions and solutions to the problems they faced. They depended on me and more and more I began to depend on them. I waited for them to learn the truth about me, the nature of my unfinished business with the world. They did that just about the time they were twelve. So, I waited for them to get over it and find me human again; fit to live on this earth and breathe the same rarified air they were enjoying.

In the meantime, I waited for them to learn to drive so I didn't have to take them everywhere and I waited the interminable minutes, sometimes hours, they were late getting home at night, imagining their precious bodies twisted and broken in a ditch, or ravaged and discarded by some madman, or compromised by drugs, or sex or rock and roll. Things that would have far reaching results and waste all my careful waiting.

I waited for my fortieth birthday with a sickly smile, a fear of what lay ahead and a prayer on my lips. I still waited for the answers to life's questions to magically be written across the sky where even I couldn't miss them. I waited for the wrinkles, the sags and ravages of age to appear on my face and body. I waited for comfort, love and reward in the silence with my husband. I waited for him to notice me again. He watched football games and puttered in the garage, oblivious to my waiting games.

I waited for biopsy results and procedure results and notes from my lover's pen. I waited for my children's visits and calls from their little corners of the world. I waited for their favor and the sharing of their lives. My bread had been cast upon the water and I waited and watched daily for its return. I read the obits religiously and waited to see my name.

I held my mother's hand and waited for her to die in a room that stifled my breath and softened my heart to mush that she had to go before I was ready. Before I'd had time to be kind enough and to understand who she was. I waited for the tears to stop.

I waited to hear, I waited to know, I waited my life away. It was all there in the photo, in the pointing of my fingers and the scuffing of my baby shoes. The miles I would travel and the waiting I would do. Waiting to know and be known, to love and be loved, to grow and be grown. Now I wonder what I've been waiting for. Waiting to die or waiting to live.

Adults R Us

*"Old age isn't so bad
when you consider the alternative."*

Pearl S. Buck

Sex and the Old Lady

JUST KIDDING!

If your husband or significant other is still living, your chance of continuing to have a satisfying sexual relationship are much better than if you are a widow.

Duh!

It's like being seventeen again and wondering if you will ever find a suitable partner. "Will I ever get to have sex?" which is a deep and lovely mystery question. Except that as an old lady the question is, "Will I ever get to have sex, again?"

Most days it looks to me like the answer is, "NO."

"Sex is like Bridge"
"If you don't have a good partner,
you'd better have a good hand."

Mae West

"I know nothing about sex
because I was always married."

Zsa Zsa Gabor

Triumphant Aging
People who kept on truckin'

Colonel Harland Sanders started Kentucky Fried Chicken at the age of sixty-five. He was almost dead broke when he began selling franchises and nine years later he sold his share of the business for 2 million dollars. He said, *"I've only had two rules…Do all you can and do it the best you can."*

Laura Ingalls Wilder began writing at the age of sixty-five. She is responsible for *The Little House on the Prairie* series of books that later became a hit television series. She said of herself, *"I've always been a busy person, doing my own housework, helping the Man of the Place when help could not be obtained; but I loved to work, and it is a pleasure to write. And, oh, I do just love to play!"*

Mary DeLaney invented the paper collage at 72 years of age. In the following ten years she created 985 botanically correct collages. King George III was such a fan he provided her housing at Windsor Castle till his death.

Estelle Getty became a co-star in the *Golden Girls* at age 63. Her words of wisdom for us are, *"Age does not bring you wisdom; age brings you wrinkles."*

Grandma Moses became folk artist at 78. She appeared on the cover of *Time Magazine* in 1952 at the age of 92. She says, *"If I hadn't started painting I would have raised chickens."*

Peter Roget invented *Roget's Thesaurus* at age 73. It has never been out of print since then. He suffered from OCD and making lists calmed his anxieties.

Edmond Hoyle began collecting rules of card games in 1741. He was 70 when he started. He said, *"When in doubt win the trick."*

Fauja Singh ran his first marathon race at age 89. He ran for 19 years after that and became the oldest man to complete a marathon at age 100.

Frank McCourt became a best-selling author and won a Pulitzer Prize for *Angela's Ashes* at 66. He said, *"You never have the same experience twice"*.

The Barber Pole

Helen and I were off the beaten path in the West Virginia mountains when I saw it. The red and white cylinder wasn't turning and the glass surrounding the cylinder was grey with coal dust or whatever silty substance clogs the air, then settles over life in coal mining country. But other than that, it was perfect and still attached to the weathered front of the clapboard building in downtown Marlinton Furnace. The downtown area was less than a block long and had a restaurant with a sign that said *GOOD EATS* in fading black letters above a grimy window sporting red and white calico café curtains.

The town was situated in a level spot surrounded by scraggly, rock-covered hills dotted with misshapen pine trees. If the town had been a man, he would be a derelict, perhaps a wino. But there in the midst of it all was the antique barber pole, just the sort of hoped for discovery that had us combing the mountain back roads in the first place. I was sure it would bring $5,000 at auction.

I pulled my white Caddy off the road and onto the combination parking area and walkway that lay between the road and the building. Gravel pinged the front of the building as I braked to a stop.

"Looks like it's going to rain," my wife said. "Don't be long." She cast a worried look toward the sky. Dark thunderheads were drifting into the small piece of sky visible between the wizened peaks that surrounded us. She was right, the sky looked threatening and I watched as the clouds threw the entire town into shadow.

"I'll hurry," I promised and stepped through the wide-open door of the barber shop. The smell of bay rum, hair oil and nicotine hung in the pre-storm air. A yellowed sign on the wall announced a haircut was still $2.00 and a shave was just fifty cents. The barber stood behind an antique leather chair slowly stropping a razor that would bring no less than a thousand dollars at auction. He was gray and so thin he might have been hollow.

"What'll it be?" he asked over the rhythmic thwap, thwap, thwap of the blade against leather.

"I don't need a haircut, actually," I said. "I'm interested in the barber pole out front."

"It's broke," he said. "Motor burned up about a year ago." He examined the blade and ran a knobby, knuckled finger along the edge, pursed his lips and looked at me through squinting yellow eyes. "How about a shave?"

"I don't think so, really, but I'd give you $75.00 for the pole."

He tilted his head and smiled, revealing tobacco brown teeth. "The barber pole is broke."

I pulled my wallet from my back pocket and began counting out bills. "I can fix it," I said.

"You a barber?" the old man asked. He flicked the barber cape over the chair raising bits of hair from previous cuts,

"I used to be." I smiled in what I hoped was an engaging manner.

"I'm thinking of retiring, too." He patted the cracked leather of the chair. "Have a seat."

I hesitated, looked through the open door at my wife, who was reading a magazine in the car. A dark rumble of thunder prowled the sky. I climbed into the old man's chair.

"If you retire, you won't need the pole," I said.

"Town's about gone anyway. The mines are played out; the EPA and the flood back in 88."

"So, you might sell it?"

"I could be persuaded."

He billowed the cape over my body and hooked it around my neck. "I could go as high as ninety dollars," I said.

"You'd have to take it down and it's been up there for more'n fifty years."

"I've got tools in my trunk."

The old man twirled me around till I was facing the mirror. My reflection looked almost as gray as his in the old glass. "So," he said. "What'll it be?"

"A little trim around the ears, I guess."

"Ninety dollars for a broke barber pole." He shook his head and began trimming hair that had a sixty-dollar styling two days earlier.

When he finished, I handed him two dollars and asked again about the pole.

"A city man willing to pay that much for a broke pole is nuts or that old pole is worth more than I think." He brushed the wisps of hair he'd just cut off my head from the chair. "How about a hundred fifty dollars.

I counted the money into his hand and hurried outside. The sky was black with clouds. Helen was standing beside the car, her arms folded tightly across her chest. "I thought you were going to hurry,' she said. She scowled and pointed a tense finger at the sky.

"I'm hurrying. I am hurrying!" I retrieved my tools from the trunk and began trying to remove the barber pole from the weathered wood. It was attached by rusty, thread-less screws. Heavy layers of white paint that long ago had worn off the building but clung stubbornly to the pole's frame. I noticed the word Duncan printed on the bottom of the pole but didn't take time to look for other signs of authenticity. It might be worth $8000.

"It's going to storm," Helen said. There was a note of hysteria in her tone.

I was working hard and fast. The humid air kept the perspiration from evaporating off my body. It ran off my forehead into my eyes and down my back. I stabbed my palm with a screwdriver trying to pry the base of the pole loose from the wood.

"Damn," I said and rubbed my hand against my trousers. It hurt, and blood began to rush to the surface and create a bruise under the skin.

"What do you think you're doing?" a man shouted from the café across the street. He stood holding the front door open with two others standing behind him, watching. There was menace in his tone.

"Tell him I've bought the pole," I said to Helen. She shook her head and hard little pellets of hail the size of marbles began to fall.

"Tell him yourself." She climbed into the car and slammed the door with an angry humph.

The three men from the café walked over to get a closer look. "Does Cletus know you're taking the pole?" one of them asked.

"Of course he knows. Assuming Cletus is your barber. I paid him a hundred fifty dollars."

"That poles been there my whole life," the younger one said.

"I don't like city folks coming through and carting off my town." The third man said.

The men were thin, sharp boned and gray just like the barber. They stood so close I could smell the stale odor of French fries and motor oil clinging to their clothes. Hail pelted them as they stood. None of them gave an inch. I tried pulling the pole loose with the claw end of my hammer. I felt the wood give a bit and an angry looking wasp flew out from behind the base. It circled my head and flew toward the trio standing too close.

"Got a wasp nest behind it," the younger man said. He stepped back a foot and smiled. "Did you buy the wasp's nest, too?"

The three men laughed. I pulled harder with the claw hammer and the screws screeched as the wood gave. Rain hadn't begun to fall in earnest yet, but wind twirled the pine trees on the hill above town. White balls of ice littered the ground. Three angry wasps circled my head.

Helen cracked her window and shouted. "Forget it Harry. Let's get out of here."

"I already paid for this and it's a Duncan," I shouted back. I slapped the wasps with my injured hand.

"Best thing to do with a wasp nest is burn it," one of the men said.

I could hear the frenzied buzz of the insects behind the barber pole. It was loosened but not yet free of the building. The wasps were going to swarm on me when I pulled it loose. I cringed at the thought.

"I saw a man die once from wasp stings," the younger man said. The wind from the storm was flapping their pants legs around their ankles by this time and the trees on the hills were bent double.

I gauged the distance from the side of the building to the door of my car. I'd never make it ahead of the wasps. The nest might even be attached to the base of the pole. The men were still standing between me and the car. They leaned back on their heels against the wind and smiled. The wind raised dust devils from the side of the road and the wasps hummed their discontent.

The barber materialized in the doorway of the shop. "It's blowing up a gully washer," he said.

"You sold your pole?" the young man asked.

"It's broke. The city man still thought it was worth a hundred fifty bucks." All four of the men laughed.

"Wasps," I said. "I need a torch."

~ 47 ~

"Yep," the barber said. He leaned against the frame of the open door.

I stepped away from the pole, walked to the car and pulled open Helen's door. "Have you lost your mind?" she said. "Those men are frightening me. It's going to pour any second. "We've got to get out of here."

"Give me your magazine," I said.

"Harry this is dangerous. . ." I reached across her body and grabbed the Modern Maturity she had been reading and hurried back to the barber pole. I turned so my back was a shield to the wind. I held my lighter to the pages of the magazine. Flames shot up, and before the wind and rain could put it out, I pulled out the pole and stuck the flaming pages under its base.

"He's going to burn down the building 'fore he's done," one of the men said.

"Could be," said the barber.

I held the frame of the pole tight against the wall and could feel the heat of the burning magazine spread to the metal base. It burned the tips of my fingers. I bit my lip against the pain and prayed the rickety old building wouldn't go up in flames. It began to rain in earnest just as I pulled the ancient Duncan barber pole free of the building. The torch had only left a black mark on the wood and had chased the wasps out of the space.

I lugged the pole and my tools to my Caddy, flipped open the trunk and stowed them all. The men followed closely, in my personal space, muttering under their breath. The wind whistled through the gully and the rain pelted us hard. I slammed the trunk shut and jumped into the car. I was soaked and a shiver ran through me.

The men stood outside my window as I floored the Caddy, grateful to be leaving Marlinton Furnace with my prize and my life. Rain washed over the car. Helen sighed beside me. I looked into my rear-view mirror and saw the three men were slapping one another on the back and having a rollicking good laugh in the downpour as Cletus lifted another barber pole to the wall of his weathered barbershop.

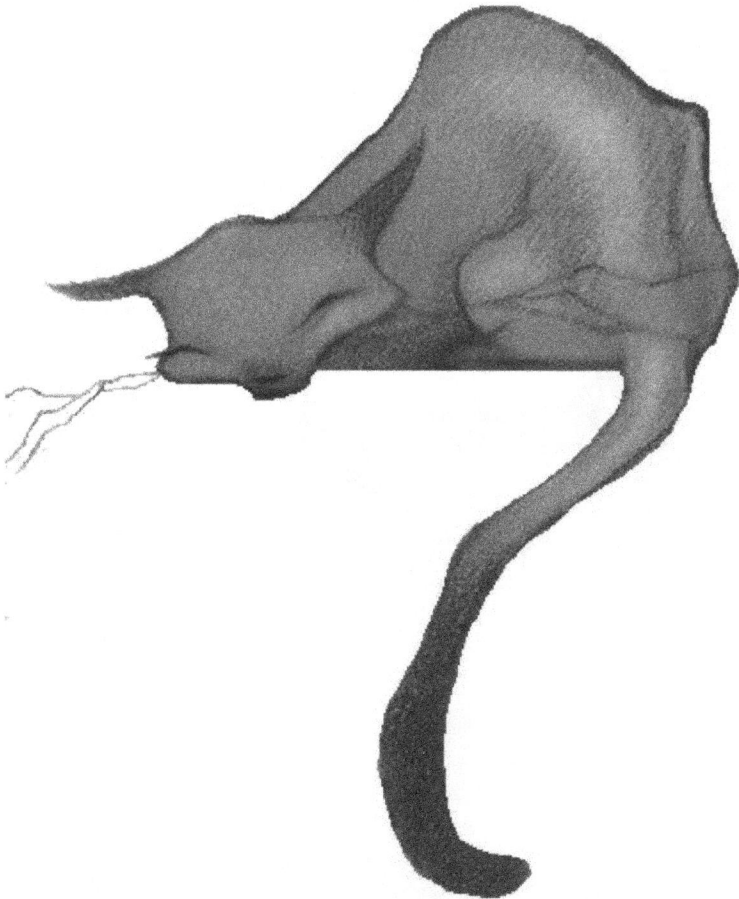

*"Old age is like a plane flying through a storm.
Once you're aboard,
there's nothing you can do about it."*

Golda Meir

Phyliss Diller Said...

"Whatever you look like, marry a man your own age. As your beauty fades, so will his eyesight."

"A bachelor is a guy who never made the same mistake once."

"Housework can't kill you, but why take a chance?"

"Cleaning your house while your kids are still growing up is like shoveling the sidewalk before it stops snowing."

"Most children threaten to run away from home. This is the only thing that keeps some parents going."

"Burt Reynolds once asked me out. I was in his room."

"The only time I ever enjoyed ironing was the day I accidently got vodka in the steam iron."

"Old age is when the liver spots show through your gloves."

"What I don't like about office Christmas parties is looking for a job the day after."

"You know you're old if they have discontinued your blood type."

A Song

Lyrics by Donnalou Stevens
Generously donated to the world on the Internet

Well, I ain't sixteen, not a beauty queen
My eyes are baggin' and my skin is saggin'
And if that's the reason you don't love me,
Maybe that's not love.

I ain't twenty either and I don't care neither,
My hair is gray and I like it that way,
And if that's the reason that you don't love me,
Maybe that's not love.

If you don't think I rock,
well we aren't going to roll.
If you don't think I hung the moon,
My hot just turned to cold.

If you wanna younger model,
I wish you well sweet pea,
Cuz if you can't see what it is you've got,
Then you ain't getting me.

I've got cellulite and achin' feet
My thighs kinda jiggle when I giggle or wiggle
And if that's the reason you don't love me,
Maybe that's not love.

My tummy ain't tucked or li-po-sucked,
It's a little poochy, but I still Hootchy Kootchy
And if that's the reason you don't love
Maybe that's not love.

See, I'm no longer desperate.
I'll only have a man
If he's got the smarts to see
How HOT that I still am.

If you want a younger model,
I wish you well sweet pea
Cuz, if you can't see what it is you have,
You ain't having me.

Older ladies, older ladies, older ladies
Are DEVINE!!!

Well, I got saggy breasts that droop from my chest.
Purt near all the way down to my nest,
And if that's the reason you don't love me,
Maybe that's not love.

I gotta a chicken neck and I love it, by heck,
It makes a double chin whenever I grin
And if that's the reason you don't love me,
Maybe that's not love.

If you don't think I rock, well we ain't gonna roll.
If you don't think I hung the moon,
My hot just turned to cold.
If you wanna younger model,
I wish you well sweet pea.
Cuz, if you can't see what it is you've got,
Then you ain't getting me.

The Birthday Gift

Long life makes a friend of death. Last night the family celebrated my eighty-sixth birthday and this morning Juniper served my breakfast on the terrace. The air is cool, fresh, fertile, feeling of spring. It caresses my arms, mingles with soft hairs there, creating goose-flesh and reminding me of the best days of my life, all of them . . . decades ago. High school graduation . . . the day I married Grady . . . the days the twins were born.

Memory is sweet. I imagine being a girl again, slipping off my shoes and feeling the dew-damp grass between my toes. Instead, I adjust the mohair throw across my lap, ring the bell on my breakfast tray and lean back into the cushioned wicker chair.

Juniper's mahogany face appears so quickly I know she's been waiting around the corner, watching me. "You finish your breakfast already, Miz Ellen?"

"I'm not hungry this morning, Juni." She flutters and clucks about me. I smile at her affected Mammy behavior. When she disapproves and feels she can't say so outright, she even lapses into dialect. I'm not supposed to notice.

"You gots to eat, Miz Ellen. Put some meat on yo' skinny little bones. You hardly safe out in a breeze these days."

"Food isn't going to fix what ails me. Has Mr. Arnold phoned yet?"

"That no account lawyer not fit for anything but crow food, Miz Ellen. Why you lettin' him trifle in your business?" Juniper Smith's eye flash like knives in the sun.

"He comes when I call, Juni. He has time to sit with an old woman like me. He keeps up with the gossip from the State House. He's Grady's cousin's boy. That reason enough?"

"He's no boy, Miz Ellen. He's fifty if he's a day and he's too smooth by a mile to be an honest man." Juniper ha-rumps and rustles about rearranging my tray. "Just try this toast. It's the good Hawaiian bread you like. I made it myself."

"Thank you, no. Just take it away and when Mr. Arnold arrives bring him out."

Juniper lifts the tray off the table, says "Yes 'um," and is gone, defeated for the moment.

***

Life becomes a burden eventually. It doesn't lose its beauty, but its ability to surprise and delight. My infirmities are a humiliation. My eyesight is failing me. Today and yesterday mingle in my mind till it's hard for me to keep them straight. I'll think I'm playing with the twins, have a flash of something I want to tell Grady, turn my head toward his chair and only then remember he's ten years in his grave. The girls are grown and gone, grandmothers themselves. Time isn't a straight line any more. I find myself floating between the times of my life with nothing "real" to anchor me in the present. It frightens me, but I think I manage to hide it from Juniper. I'm afraid she will call in some specialist and have him try to rescue me – as if a person can be cured of old age.

***

"Mr. Arnold's here," Juniper announces from the wide open double door. Hap Arnold stands beside her, his hat in one hand, his briefcase in another.

"Hap," I extend my hand. "I won't get up." Hap laughs politely. I haven't walked for six months and the joke is getting old.

"You're looking wonderful, Ellen." He takes my hand and bows from the waist to kiss it. It is a well-bred lie and I accept it.

"Would you like some tea? A cup of coffee?" I ask.

"A whiskey perhaps if it's not against house rules."

I nod. "Bring Mr. Arnold a whiskey, Juni."

"Will Mister be staying for lunch?" she asks. Her disapproval oozing between the words.

"We'll tend to that later," I say. She turns on her heel and leaves. Hap takes a seat across the patio table from me, lays his hat on an empty chair and sets his briefcase on the floor.

"She doesn't like me much," he says.

"She's protective of me. It's nothing personal."

Juniper brings the whiskey decanter, ice and a glass for Hap. She puts it on the table with her nose narrowed and her shoulders stiffly set. Then she returns to the doorway prepared to stand guard. "Thank you, Juniper," I say. "That will be all."

Hap raises his eyebrows at the angry flap of her shoes as she leaves. He pours himself a glass of whiskey and asks. "Do you mind if I smoke?" He pulls a cigar from his vest pocket.

"Not at all. Cigar smoke and whiskey remind me of Grady – men things. It makes me feel young again. Now tell me what is happening in town."

Hap concentrates on the cigar till it's lit, then leans back in his chair and begins the tales of business and political intrigue. They are stories Grady and I would have been players in twenty years before.

Grady made a fortune in construction in the fifties and sixties. He did good work for a fair price and in the beginning, I answered the phone and kept the books. We worked hard and made the right connections to keep the contracts coming our way through three administrations. Grady invested well and by the time the girls were in high school, we had more money than we could ever spend. I was able to stay home, and we had long vacations skiing and flying off to sunshiny islands in the warm sea. It was idyllic. I never loved anyone but Grady – not even for a moment. I'm not sure about Grady, but if he had other women, he never hurt me by it. Our lives were good. I like thinking about it now it's over as much as I liked living it when it happened. But all that's really left is the money.

"How was the party last night?" Hap asks.

"Gala," I say. 'Five generations were here, if you count the babies."

Hap sips his whiskey. "You have to count the babies."

"I suppose so. They were powdered and pink, wiggly and wet. Their parents put them on my knees and hovered nearby, hoping the dutiful visits will result in a trust fund."

"How many are there now?"

"Three of them." I shake my head. "My great-great grandchildren stumping for their lunch."

Hap laughs. "An interesting point of view."

"It would be funny, if it weren't so sad," I say. "If I could remember who they are."

Hap's laughter fades. He sips his whiskey, doesn't meet my eyes.

"Did you bring the papers?"

"You've decided then?"

"Yes. I decided last night after the party. It will be my birthday gift to me."

Hap nods. "If you're sure." He pulls a folder from his briefcase, lays it on the table and hands over a gold pen. "You really should read them before you sign."

"My eyes," I say. "You read it to me."

He flips open the folder and begins to read the contract that specifies my wish for a painless, easy death at the hands of Dr. Angelo Valequez. When he finishes, he passes the papers to me and I sign them.

"And here's the authorization for the transfer of funds to Dr. Valequez's account in Guatemala."

I sign it, too.

"Who says money can't buy everything," Hap says. He pours more whiskey and chugs it back.

"It can't buy me love, or Grady's return," I say. "It can't buy me anything that would make me want to go on living. It's just buying me some measure of control. If I were willing to give that up, I could get Dr. Valequez's gift for nothing, eventually."

"Death and taxes," Hap says with a wry smile.

Hap lays his hand on mine. "I have to go." His glass is empty, his eyes are red.

"Can I have Juniper bring you a sandwich?"

"I have three more calls to make," he says. "Four clients for Dr. Valequez this trip. He'll fly in the night before, see his patients and be back in Guatemala that same evening."

"You work too hard, Hap. You have to eat. I'll have Juniper bring you something." I ring the bell, but he is already standing with his hat in his hand by the time Juniper appears.

"I guess Mr. Arnold is leaving," I say. "Will you show him out?"

Juniper eyes the half empty whiskey bottle; Hap's red rimmed eyes. "He can't find his own way?" she says and heads for the door.

Hap bends to kiss my cheek before he leaves. His lips are dry. I can smell the whiskey and the cigar smoke. I think of Grady.

"See you next week," he says. "Dr. Valequez will be with me."

"I'll be ready.

"Life is sexually transmitted and the Mortality Rate is 100%"

R.D. Laing

Nobody's Perfect

The year I graduated high school there were only 99 elements on the periodic table. It was one of the last easy years. You know, the years before Viet Nam, Kent State, Nixon's resignation, 3 Mile Island, Madonna and other national disgraces.

I tell you this to place myself in time, so you'll know I was the good guy. It wasn't me who started it. It was George. He came home from work one day and ended my life as I knew it.

"I need some space, Marge," he said. Tears sprung into his eyes as he spoke. I have to give him credit for that. His shoulders sloped and his chin jutted forward in the way I found especially annoying.

"Space?" I said stopping half-way between the stove and the kitchen table. "What do you mean space?"

Only his eyes didn't lower and continued to gaze at me from an odd angle.

"Trapped?" I continued to the table and set the pasta bowl down. My eyes never left his as I tossed the fettuccine with the marinara sauce. The heat escaping from the bowl crept up my arms as I worked. I forced the corners of my mouth upward and felt tautness of my upper lip against my teeth.

George lifted his head to look at me and I could no longer see the vulnerable spot on top where the hair was thinning and skin peeked through. He let his own lips experiment with a smile. "I thought you'd be upset."

"What exactly are you planning to do?" I asked continuing to toss the fettuccine.

He leaned forward, his eyes twinkling as he warmed to my question. "Well, I've rented a little place over on Summit Square, just two bedrooms and no garage, but it's clean and there's a patio." My husband of twenty-six years leaned back into his chair and smiled full out.

"Hmmm." I said lowering my eyes to the bowl which looked suddenly full of pale squirming snakes.

"You're being a sport about this, Marge. I really appreciate it." He was beaming 150 watts by this time.

"What about me, George?" I asked.

"It'll be a new beginning for both of us. You'll have to get a job, of course. But you'll meet new people and do new things . . .like water skiing."

He paused thoughtfully, foolishly. "Remember you always wanted to water ski and couldn't because I hated water. It won't be a problem anymore."

"I'm forty-eight years old, George. Not a prime age to start water skiing."

"You're never too old to start or to learn. Never!" He looked briefly like the young man I'd married, full of hope, full of promise for the future.

I didn't think. I didn't hesitate. I dumped the entire bowl of still-steaming pasta in his lap.

He jumped to his feet sending squirming snakes to the floor. I backed up to lean against the stove. 'Jeez," he yelled, hopping up and down and swiping at his crotch. "Hot!" He grabbed a napkin and wiped furiously at the front of his pants. "Why'd you do that? Dammit, Marge. Why'd you do that?"

He unbuckled his pants and started to pull them down.

"I wouldn't do that if I were you," I said.

He paused long enough to see the look on my face, then gingerly pulled the fabric away from his skin. I could see the steam escape as he did it. It warmed my soul.

***

"He brought her to dinner, Mom," Tracy said. There was a sharp intake of breath before she went on. "She's only twenty-six. Just five years older than me and dad couldn't keep his hands off her." I heard sniffling and switched the phone over to my other ear. "It was so gross, I thought I would die."

I let her cry a little before responding. "It's his life, Tracy. He can live it however he wants."

"But Mom, what about me?" Sniff. Sniff. "He says I have to start thinking about paying my own tuition. Sniff. Sniff. His funds are short."

"It'll be ok, Honey. Just different for a while. You've only got a year to go. We'll work it out."

"I'll come home if you want."

"No need for that, Tracy. Tuition is paid for the semester. We'll work it out."

***

My first job was as a doctor's receptionist. My pay was just over half the monthly expenses for the house. My attorney suggested we ask for the house to be sold as part of the settlement.

She was smart and sympathetic; a 32-year-old woman who had never been married. "In my line of work, you see too much," she said. "Trust becomes a very tough issue."

"I imagine it does." We talked over a glass of wine she bought after my first day in court.

"Single suits me fine." She raised her eyebrows and sipped her wine.

"I don't remember single," I sighed. "It was so long ago."

"Like riding a bike, I hear." She laughed at her own little joke.

***

He was Carolyn Ferguson's brother-in-law, a widower and recently retired.

"I'm not sure I'm ready for this," I said to Tracy. Who was home for spring break.

"It'll be fun, Mom. She stood back, tilted her head to one side and examined my hair. She was helping me get it just right. "How long's it been since you had a real date?"

"Hmmm? About twenty-seven years, I think."

Tracy smiled and smoothed another wisp of hair. "It'll come back to you."

"I don't know. It's been a long time and he seems so old. Sixty-three, Tracy. Almost as much difference as your dad and Gwen."

"Gwen is a tart, just taking advantage of dad's . . . confusion.'

I had to smile at her view of George's situation.

"Things are different these days." She tilted her head in the other direction. "You have to be careful." Her eyes leveled on mine. "You know, like safe sex and all."

"It's our first date," I laughed. "No need to worry about any sex at all. Besides he's sixty-three."

I smiled, nodded and heard about the new birds and bees from my daughter.

***

The reorganization of a life takes some time, like additions to the periodic table and mine was going nicely by the day George came home. I'd found a job that allowed me to pay the bills. A for sale sign decorated the front lawn and I had a package of condoms in the zipper compartment of my purse, just in case.

His shoulders sloped, his chin jutted forward as he stood on the porch of our former home. If he wore a hat, it would have been in his hand. "She's left me," he said.

"Hmmmm," I answered.

"She made me feel young, Marge. Like I could have another ride on the merry-go-round." George raised his eyes to meet mine. "I hate seeing the "For Sale" sign in our yard." He gestured with a loosely flung arm.

"A young couple with two children are interested," I said. "I think they're going to make an offer."

His eyelids slid closed. "I've made a mess of everything, haven't I?"

"Well, I could always make another batch of fettuccine with marinara."

"Would you?"

~ 65 ~

I crossed my arms over my bosom in a protective gesture and leaned back against the door frame. "Trust is a big issue with me these days."

"Yes, I suppose it is."

"I've met some new people and I like my job. I even joined a sailing club."

George's head bent forward and I could see new skin peeping through the thin spot on top. "What about me?" he muttered.

"Think of it as a new beginning, George," I said with a smile.

"What would old ladies be without old men?"

Diana Forrester

Bob Hope Said...

On turning 70: *"I still chase women, but only downhill."*

On turning 80: *"Even your birthday suit needs pressing."*

On turning 90: *"The candles cost more than the cake."*

On turning 100: *"I don't feel anything till noon and then it's time for my nap."*

On never winning an Oscar: *"At my house we call the Academy Awards, "Passover".*

The Scary Stuff

"Wish I had time for one more bowl of chili."

Dying words of Kit Carson

A Daisy Chain of Woes

Barbara Jones hadn't lived a long life yet. A pity really, because Barbara enjoyed life and had been looking forward to more of it when she took a nasty fall while biking down Honeybaker's Hill last Tuesday evening. It was a set of odd and unusual circumstances that laid her up in the hospital right next door to death.

Her biking helmet wasn't where she always left it and she hated those things anyway. Barbara believed things like biking helmets were allowing too many stupid people to contribute to the gene pool. That's what half of modern life was about; protecting stupid people. People too dumb to stay upright on their bikes or too stupid to keep hot coffee out of their crotch. People too stupid to be part of the human race. Her daughter, Judith Ann, had bought the bike helmet for her and so she wore it, but when it came up missing she had no motivation to search for it.

She started on her ride without it and just as she was picking up speed down Honeybaker's Hill, a huge black dog raced out of a stand of pine trees straight into the front wheel of her Cannondale snapping the dog's neck and toppling Barbara ass over elbows onto the blacktop of the road. The fall broke Barbara's right leg and sent a blood clot scorching a path from her ankle to her head like a bullet train screaming through her veins and her not quite sixty. She became a stupid victim though she'd already made her contribution to the gene pool. And not such a wonderful one it was; a daughter, a son and assorted grandchildren aged twelve to twenty-one. She's taught them all to compete fiercely and to look out for number one. It was the way of the modern world.

She should be dead by now. All the doctors said so. The family had been in and hovered around her bed, children uncharacteristically silent as if her impending death had zipped their lips. They'd moved her three times since Tuesday. Each time into a less medically supportive environment. The goal was to see if she could sustain her own life. Smart money was on the side of her death. But she was laying now in a regular hospital bed with her head slightly elevated. The only life support was a tube of sugar water running into her arm and a urine tube running out from you guess where. Barbara wasn't ready to die yet and inside the husk of her body she seemed to have some control over what happened.

It was true she couldn't wiggle her pinkie finger or blink her eyelids, but she was as alive and alert inside as she had ever been. The pesky arthritic pain in her knees was gone. In fact, Barbara decided she had never felt so good. Well, not for years at any rate. Maybe since her children were born. Maybe since Maurice went out for smokes and never came back. She wasn't sure about that part, but she could hear and see everything and nobody out there suspected.

It was a bit unsettling that the world appeared and disappeared without her being able to move so much as her eyes to follow the action but once she got the hang of it, Barbara thought it was exciting really.

Judith Ann came into Barbara' view first. Judith Ann had been a quiet child and time had turned her into a disagreeable adult. Her eyebrows made a dark ridge across her face and she had a stern look about her. Looks were more important for a girl and Barbara had always thought Judith Ann's looks were as much a handicap as blindness or a missing limb might be. On the other hand, Judith Ann had always been loyal and for this reason Barbara had chosen her to be her right hand in the mail order business she started after Maurice left her and the children to their own devices. The business had succeeded financially better than Maurice had ever done and it hadn't taken long for Barbara to realize his disappearance was just what she had needed to stimulate her own creativity and ability to perform.

Judith Ann tipped darkly into her mother's view and stared down at Barbara with her unfortunate ridge of eyebrow wiggling erratically. "Mother," Judith Ann said tentatively, then more assertively, "Mother, look what you've done by not wearing your helmet."

From the far side of the room Barbara could hear Maurice Jr., "She can't hear you Judy. Doc Harris says there is no brain activity at all."

"There are things I need to say Maury, whether she can hear them or not. She's left me with the stockholder's meeting coming up and no clear direction about what to do."

"You'll figure it out, you always do. You always have."

Barbara could only see the side of Judith Ann's head for the moments she turned to speak to Maurice, then she turned back and stared sternly down at her mother before moving out of Barbara's view. Barbara concentrated with all her might and tried moving her eyeballs to follow the path Judith Ann took but it was no good, Maurice began pacing the room and she could see his dark hair going back and forth, bouncing slightly as he walked.

"Are you going to call father?" Maurice asked.

"Do you think I should?" Judith Ann said.

Maurice's head stopped bouncing as he ceased pacing. "Father? Are you going to call father?" Barbara couldn't believe her ears. She wanted to stand on the bed and scream but of course she couldn't.

She could see the movement of Maurice's head resume. "I don't know," he said.

Judith Ann's face popped into Barbara's view blocking out Maurice's head for a moment. "She's not dead yet. They've removed every bit of life support and surely she can't hold on much longer."

"Having father show up here might jolt her back to life," Maurice Jr. said. "Are you prepared to take that chance?"

Barbara strained, tried to see the look on Maurice's face, nothing worked. It sounded like Maurice was happy she was near death.

"Nothing could suit me better," Judith Ann said. "I hate the thought of having to deal with the shareholders all alone."

Barbara was straining to move her eyeballs, straining to make sense of the conversation, not feeling nearly so good as she thought she had felt only moments before. Father? What the hell are they talking about?

"You think it would be easier to deal with mother, if she knew we'd been in touch with father all these years?"

"I can handle mother," Judith Ann said. "I always have."

Barbara stared at the ceiling only because she had no choice. No choice at all. She was trapped.

"I wish you'd waited to set this up," Judith Ann said. 'Mother would have had the stockholder's reports nearly done in two more days."

Set this up? Set what up? Barbara was trying to make sense where none existed.

"I never do anything that suits you, do I?" Maurice said.

"The stockholders will never accept father as the new head of the company just on my say so."

"They won't have any choice," Maurice said. "With mother gone we hold all the aces."

Judith Ann bent over her mother again and stared into her face. "Mother's not gone yet," she said. Barbara could feel a splatter of saliva as Judith Ann spoke. She wanted to reach up and grab Judith Ann and demand to know what she and Maurice were up to.

"She can't last much longer," Maurice said.

"She should have died when they unhooked the machines," Judith Ann said.

"That's what Dr. Harris was afraid of."

"He was too optimistic, wasn't he?"

Maurice moved into Barbara's line of sight. He put a finger to his chin. A thoughtful look overtook him. "By a mile, there are no plugs left to pull. We have to depend on nature taking its course now."

"Nobody suspects us of a thing," Judith Ann said. "We could try something else."

"A second attempt on mother's life would be too suspicious."

"Nobody has a clue there's even been one attempt on mother's life."

Barbara listened as tears welled in her eyes but her body no longer had the ability to release them. Surely her children had tried to kill her and nearly succeeded. Surely the biking accident was no accident and Maurice had been in touch with the children for some time.

"The stock won't pass to us till she's dead," Judith Ann said. "You have to finish the job, Maury."

"I have to finish the job? Why is it always me? I hid the helmet, I trained the dog to go hell bent after the rabbit scent I gobbed on her tires. I hid in the pine grove and watched to see it all happened as planned. I've done enough."

Barbara agreed. Maurice had done more than his share. Both of her children leaned over her bed. Judith Ann on the right, Maurice on the left. They lifted their eyes and looked at one another. "We can't leave her like this," Judith Ann said.

Barbara lay helplessly, watching.

"I've done all I'm going to do," Maurice said and stepped back out of Barbara's sight. "Another attempt could land me in prison and I won't take that chance."

"Nothing changes till we control a majority of the stock."

Barbara controlled 51 percent. She had been wise to keep that for herself. Well, if you didn't consider that her having control is what started this chain of events. If you could overlook the fact that her children had planned her death in order to gain control.

Doctor Harris came into the room. He was a tall man, dark haired and good looking. He nodded at Maury and Judith Ann before going straight to Barbara. She could see him as he spoke. "We've had the least desirable outcome from our treatment. Your mother's vital signs are strong. She can survive like this for years." Barbara tried blinking. She tried shaking her head. She screamed a scream only she could hear.

"How likely is that?" Judith Ann asked. Her brow got darker and thicker as she spoke.

"How likely is what?" Dr. Harris asked.

"That she will go on like this for years."

Dr. Harris studied Barbara's children. His lips narrowed and his eyes darted from one to the other. "Very likely," he said at last. "This is the there are worse things than death scenario. Your mother could literally live like this for the rest of her life. Another eighteen years if she lives the normal life span for a woman her age."

"Here in the hospital?" Judith Ann asked.

"No. We'll move her to a nursing home."

"Are there any other options?" Judith Ann asked.

The three of them were gathered around Barbara's bed and all were in her view. "Are you thinking of using her for a door stop?" Maurice asked.

Dr. Harris stepped back from the bed. "That isn't even funny," he said, out of Barbara's view. "But that's about all she'll be good for."

"Any chance she'll regain consciousness?" Judith Ann asked with a stern look at her brother.

"None," the doctor said. He cleared his throat and went on. "Sometimes families decide to take matters into their own hands in these situations. Sometimes families want to help things along . . . just for the sake of the patient, of course. Even under these circumstances a death can be suspicious and I want you both to know any suspicious death is reported to the police so don't even think about it."

Judith Ann looked at Maurice Jr., he stared at his mother who gazed steadily at Judith Ann. They were stuck like this, all three of them. A daisy chain of woes.

Food for Thought

"Men are like floors. Lay them right and you can walk all over them for years."   Betsy Salkind

"When a man opens a car door for his wife, it's either a new car or a new wife."   Prince Philip

"The best cure for Sea Sickness is to sit under a tree."   Spike Milligan

"If life were fair, Elvis would still be alive and all the impersonators would be dead."   Johnny Carson

"Home cooking.   Where many a man thinks his wife is."   Jimmy Durante

"As I hurtled through space, one thought kept crossing my mind – every part of this rocket was supplied by the lowest bidder."   John Glenn

"Death is the number one killer in the world."   Anonymous

"Life is like a jar of peppers. What you do today may burn your ass tomorrow."   Roger Darlington

"In hotel rooms, I worry. I can't be the only guy who sits on the furniture naked."   Jonathan Katz

"If God had intended us to fly he would have made it easier to get to the airport."   Jonathan Winters

No Second Chances
Saturday . . . Labor Day weekend
September 3, 2000

We're burying my mother today. It's hot . . .humid . . . steaming. Hell comes to mind. I'm nervous about the service, about seeing my brother . . . about burying my mother. I put a red dress on.

We arrive early and are met by the mortician and the preacher. Four dozen assorted pink roses sit on either side of the gravestone. My father's name is there. He's been dead fourteen years. My mother's name is there, too . . . without a date of death. I will have to make arrangements for the addition. My name is there . . . and my brother's. We are united on the gravestone of our parents, but since the disagreement . . . no place else.

There is a metal urn filled with my mother's ashes. It sits on top of the green cloth camouflaging the hole in the earth. I want to cry for the finality of it, for the things not said, the chances missed. For my mother's failures and my own, but with death there are no second chances. I bite my lip and smile, making a joke with the preacher. He is suited up like it is a cool fall day . . . sweat beads on his forehead. I wonder if he thinks of Hell.

People begin to arrive. We sweat and hug, speaking softly and avoid looking at the grave. My mother's friends, my brother's friends and mine. They form a cocoon around me. They hold my clammy hand. It feels good. I can do this. I thank them for coming. Sweat trickles down my back. My brother and his family stand apart. He doesn't look at me.

I take the minister by the arm and lead him to my brother. "This is Reverend Carlisle," I say. My brother nods and doesn't say a word. The preacher extends his hand and mumbles something. My brother lifts his eyes. "Let's don't do this today," I say. "Please?" He looks back to the grass and the preacher and I return to my mother's grave.

The minister clears his throat and begins his words of comfort for those of us who are left. My mother was not a religious woman, so the words are from Ecclesiastics and the prayer is from Alcoholics Anonymous. It is a short little service and at the end we pass out the roses to everyone as a remembrance. Pink was my mother's favorite color and I remember her . . . giddy and girlish going to a dance with my father in a frothy dress of these same shades . . . when I was nine . . . when life was simple . . . and there were chances left for all of us.

My brother and I . . . we go our separate ways.

*"No one is so old
he does not think he could live another year."*

Cicero

Good Grief -Time Flies
Things we've seen and done

1943: a) Winston Churchill pledges full support to U.S. against Japan.

b) I was born.

1944: DNA is first isolated by Oswald Avery.

1945: U.S. drops atom bombs on Hiroshima and Nagasaki.

1946: The World Cup is not held.

1947: The Dead Sea Scrolls are discovered.

1948: Nation of Israel is proclaimed.

1949: The Yankees beat the Dodgers in the World Series.

1950: Charles Schultz introduces the *Peanuts* comic strip.

1951: J.D. Salinger publishes the *Catcher in the Rye.*

1952: Nelson Mandela is arrested.

1953: First Corvette is sold.

1954: Salk polio vaccine is first administered to children.

1955: Rosa Parks refuses to go to the back of the bus.

1956: Elvis Presley becomes one of the world's first rock stars.

1957: Russia launches Sputnik and the Space Age.

1958: U.S. Supreme Court rules unanimously that Little Rock Public Schools must integrate

1959: First Grammy Awards are presented.

1960: John F Kennedy defeats Richard Nixon for president.

1961: *To Kill a Mocking Bird* by Harper Lee wins a Pulitzer Prize.

1962: Johnny Carson takes over the *Tonight Show.*

1963: a) first artificial heart is transplanted by Michael De Bakey.

b) U.S. Supreme Court rules public schools cannot require recitation of the *Lord's Prayer*.

d) President Kennedy shot and killed in Dallas.

e) *Feminine Mystic* published by Betty Friedan.

1964: a) *Peyton Place* is introduced on ABC.

b) the Beatles come to America.

1965: First U.S. troops are sent to Viet Nam.

1966: Medicare begins.

1967: U.S. unemployment rate is 3.8%.

1968: a) Martin Luther King is killed.

b) Bobby Kennedy is killed.

1969: Woodstock happens.

1970: a) Four Kent State students are killed.

b) Median household income is $8,734.

1971: The 26th amendment lowers the voting age to 18.

1972: Atari introduces the arcade version of *Pong* (the first video game).

1973: a) U.S. Supreme Court rules on Roe V Wade.

b) Median household income is $10,512.

1974: Nixon resigns.

1975: Life expectancy is 72.6 years.

1976: The U.S. celebrates its bicentennial.

1977: Elvis dies at Graceland in Memphis at age 42.

1978: a) Sony introduces the Walkman, first portable stereo.

b) The first test tube baby, Louise Brown, is born in London.

1979: Three Mile Island releases radiation in a nuclear power plant accident.

1980: John Lennon of the Beatles is shot dead in New York City.

1981: a) President Ronald Reagan nominates Sandra Day O'Conner as the first woman on the Supreme Court.

b) AIDS is identified.

1982: Michael Jackson introduces *Thriller* which becomes the biggest selling album in history.

1983: Terrorist explosion kills 237 US marines in Beirut.

1984: Soviet Union withdraws from Summer Olympics in U.S.

1985: Two Shiite Muslim gunmen capture TWA airliner with 133 aboard.

1986: a) Space shuttle Challenger explodes after launch at Cape Canaveral, FL, killing all seven aboard.

b) Fox network is established.

c) Oprah Winfrey hits national TV.

1987: James Baldwin and Andy Warhol die.

1988: Pan-Am 747 explodes from a terrorist's bomb and crashes in Lockerbie, Scotland killing 270 people.

1989: a) the Berlin Wall is removed.

b) first world wide web server and browser developed.

1990: a) dissolution of the USSR.

b) Median household income is $29,943

1991: First cholera epidemic in a century attacks 100,000 and kills more than 700 in South America.

1992: a) Bush and Yeltsin proclaim the end of the Cold War.

b) Johnny Carson hosts the Tonight Show for the last time.

1993: a) five arrested in first bombing of World Trade Center.

b) first humans are cloned and then destroyed when they reach the 32-cell stage.

1994: Four are convicted in World Trade Center bombing.

1995: a) O. J. Simpson tried for murdering his wife. He is found not guilty.

b) a pair of UK doctors create the first cloned sheep.

1996: a) Unabomber is arrested.

b) 45 million people are on the Internet.

c) Ella Fitzgerald dies.

1997: J. K. Rowling's first *Harry Potter* book published in U.K.

1998: John Glenn orbits the earth a second time at the age of 77.

1999: Eric Harris and Dylan Klebold kill thirteen people at Columbine High School.

2000: U.S. soldiers on Navy destroyer *Cole* die in Yemen terrorist explosion.

2001: Four high-jacked airplanes attack Twin Towers and the Pentagon.

2002: North Korea admits developing nuclear weapons in defiance of treaty.

2003: Sadam Hussein is captured by American troops.

2004: a) huge tsunami devastates Asia. 200,000 killed.

b) first gay marriages occur in Massachusetts

2005: Hurricane Katrina devastates the Gulf coast, killing 1000 and leaving millions homeless.

2006: Pluto loses its status as a planet when the International Astronomical Union votes to redefine the solar system.

2007: Minimum wage is $5.87

2008: a) Barack Obama is the first black man to be elected president of the U.S.

b) Median household income is $50,303

2009: Michael Jackson dies

2010: Unemployment rate is 9.7%

considered living in poverty in the worst economic depression since the Great Depression.

b) U.S. troops and the CIA kill Osama bin Laden in Pakistan.

c) Kate Middleton marries Prince William.

2012: Asians, blacks, Hispanics and mixed races make just over 50% of all births becoming a majority for the first time in U.S. history.

2013: Boston Marathon bombing.

2014: Pentagon begins shrinking the U.S. Army to the smallest size it has been since WWII.

2015: Black Lives Matter comes to be.

2016: Donald Trump is elected president.

2017: Hurricane Harvey is an epic storm.

*"Life is like a roll of toilet paper.
The closer you get to the end,
the faster it goes."*

Anonymous

The Crone's Lament

I was married twice, widowed twice and am now alone, but I have seen many things. Men falling to their knees wrenched by love before the blue-veined beauty of pale white skin.

It doesn't last.

I am a mother many times but only two of my bairns survived their birth and them feebly so, till my cradle is emptied.

Joy is fleeting. Tears eternal.

I worked and prayed and tended my garden in its season, but drought and wind and blazing sun browned it all.

God, why me?

Then I lay with many men, sighing with feigned delight, opening wide but never pierced by love again. Many came but no one stayed.

Now I am old, with whiskered chin and warty hands, veins still blue but bulging forth with graveyard dancing.

It is my future.

I dress in black and hug the shadows when I venture out. Children cry and turn their eyes; mothers rush them from the clatter of my bones.

I expect no more.

I've had my way with life, and it with me. My pulse is slowed and hot breath gone.

I wonder what it was all about.

The Really Scary Stuff

"Don't let it end like this.
Tell them I said something."

Dying words of Pancho Villa

Reflections on Death

Jimmy _____ is the first person I knew who died. I was fourteen and so was he, freshmen in high school. My family had moved (again) that year, my father was chasing a secure and well-paying job that fit what he thought he was worth with his four-year-old GI Bill engineering degree.

I was chagrined and angry to be leaving the home town I knew. My parents humored me by allowing me to spend most of the summer with my grandmother in that same home town. She allowed me to go to a drive-in movie with Jimmy (not a boyfriend but a friend who used to live next door).

Jimmy put his arm around me in the back seat of his brother's car and I laid my head on his chest. I still remember the good, strong beating as his heart tha-rumped into my ear. I listened to it; maybe the first time I really listened to the powerful beat of another person's heart. It mesmerized me to the point that I remember it now, nearly sixty years later.

It was six months later that my friend from the old home town called to tell me Jimmy had died after sneaking out of his mother's house in the middle of the night with some friends and a six pack. They didn't make the curve – the one we all called Dead Man's Curve – and ended up in a field, tossed, turned, torn apart and dead.

I had been absorbed into my new school by this time and had some new friends. I cried teenage tears for Jimmy and then I moved on. But I have had the job of carrying the tha-rump of his heart along with me throughout my life.

My grandmother was the second person in my life who died. She was tall and had big feet; not a pretty woman. My grandfather had gone on the train to Illinois to marry her and bring her back to mother his two children, whose mother had died. My grandmother was twenty-four at the time. When her husband left years later under difficult circumstances she worked hard at the canning factory in Redkey. She had a black Ford coupe she drove for years and years. It had a running board and sometimes she'd let me ride there, clinging to the car door. It was thrilling to have the wind in my hair and my skirt blowing wildly. Whenever we came across an ear of corn laying in the road, she'd stop. My job was to hop off the running board, grab the ear of corn and toss it into the front seat to take home for her chickens. (You could do that back in those days.) Sometimes if we were in the country with corn growing tall on both sides of the road, she'd coach me to pull a few extra ears from the field and toss those into the car, too.

And so it went till she was eighty. She fell one day and refused to get up again. She went to a nursing home and lived there the last six years of her life. We went to visit and took the grand kids. The staff tried coaxing her to enter walking therapy, but she refused. She lay in bed holding court with people who brought her good old butter beans (as she called them) and other culinary delights. Then she died.

I rode with my brother to the funeral in the home town we'd left so long before. It was a stormy day. There was a tornado watch. I am afraid of tornados. As my brother drove us to the burial site, I could see the low-hanging dark clouds above the house on the hill that always got hit and then rebuilt after these weather events. And yes, the clouds still hung low and dark as we twisted and twirled safely around Dead Man's Curve. My cousin was at the funeral in very proper espadrilles and it turned out I was still jealous of her after all these years. And now I knew two people who were dead.

My father had rheumatic fever as a child. The theory is that it weakened his heart and he had his first heart attack at thirty-seven. I remember being terrified. How would we survive without him?

He was big like his mother, my grandmother. He played basketball in Indiana gyms and barns in 1940 and 1941. He fell in love with my mother the first time he saw her at a skating rink some place in Indiana. Two weeks later he took her to Kentucky where they were married and nine months later, I was born.

My father had several small heart attacks during his forties and fifties. He had his own business by that time and traveled the State of Ohio. Some of his trips ended with him in an Ohio hospital. It was dicey for all of us, but time passed, he survived again and again. I got married, had children, lived my life. He and my mother lived theirs between Ohio and Florida.

It was my second son's graduation day and I got to hand out diplomas. We had a party planned for after the ceremony. When we arrived home my younger brother was there with the news that our dad had died filling up his gas tank just south of the Florida state line. "Dead before he hit the ground," my brother was told.

"What are we going to do?" my second brother asked.

"Who knows," I said. Then, "This is Scott's big day. Grandpa is not going to get any deader. I think we should go on with Scott's party and deal with this later." Which is what we all agreed to do.

After the party, my brother took our mother home with him and broke the news to her. We told the people who were staying with us. Everybody cried. It was awful. Scott was graduated, and it was time to deal with my dad. My brother took care of the business of this. He had my dad cremated and the ashes mailed to us. We scheduled his service accordingly.

Well, grandpa's ashes, the urn and everything got lost in the mail and didn't arrive in time for the funeral. He would have cussed and screamed about what a sorry situation it is when the government kept a man from getting to his own funeral on time. And that was my third death experience.

There is much reflection required around the subject of death. Trust me, I have done my share. Sometimes as we advance in age we know more people who have died than who are living. This is the way life happens. Some folks linger and suffer beyond what even makes sense; some others fall dead without a visible symptom.

That's just the way it is.

The solution (I believe) is to live every day to its fullest.

Love and appreciate your friends and family.

Let the sun shine on your face every day you can.

Take a walk in the rain.

Listen to the music that speaks to you.

Buy your bananas yellow.

Spend your money on what makes you happy.

Don't break a hip.

Laugh.

Hug your grandchildren if they will let you.

Continue to do the best you know how.

It really does matter.

You really do matter, even after you're gone.

Good Ole Bob

My friend, good ole Bob, died on Sunday. He'd eaten his lunch, was walking up the hallway to finish painting a door frame when he fell, flat on his face. Dead. He wasn't gone an hour when I got the first call.

"I have some really bad news," my friend said.

I braced myself, "What?"

"Bob had a heart attack."

"Did he die," I asked.

"Yes."

"Damn, damn, damn."

I knew I was going to miss him. I knew we were all going to miss him. I knew getting used to having him gone was going to be a chore. It had happened so suddenly. I also knew this would be happening to us more and more often. I wondered briefly which one of us would be next. Already we had lost a couple. Two of them were gone. One man had lost his wife. I'd lost my husband and now "good ole Bob" was gone.

We had reached seventy, my good friends and I. I don't know how it happened.

We became an item, actually several items, the year we turned forty. Traveling in a pack, like teenagers except that we had cars and our own money. We ate, we drank, we had strippers and we laughed. Oh dear Lord, we laughed. Those were the days my friend. We thought they would never end.

But they have. Some of us are still laughing and dancing. All of us have slowed down. We still manage to laugh a lot, but we weren't laughing Sunday. We were holding hands and hugging. Sobbing and cussing because it doesn't go on forever.

Believe it. Prepare for it. Embrace it. And laugh every time you have a chance.

We are a mist that appears for a little while and then vanishes.

Even "good ole Bob".

"Sex at ninety is like trying to shoot pool with a rope."

George Burns

Dick Davis's List

My old friend, Dick Davis, makes a new list each year of the things he has learned in his life. He read the list each year at our church talent show. He made it up to eighty and then he died. But he gave me permission to share his list in a book and this is it. I hope you enjoy.

EIGHTY THINGS I'VE LEARNED IN EIGHTY YEARS
BY RICHARD DAVIS
Printed by permission of Joyce Davis 2018

1. I know that I don't know – what I don't know.
2. Almost everything will work again if you unplug it for a few minutes, including yourself.
3. Let's face it, a nice creamy chocolate cake does a lot for a lot of people. It does for me.
4. Never laugh at your wife's choices. You are one of them.
5. Sin cannot be undone. Only forgiven.
6. Feeling gratitude and not expressing it is like wrapping a present and not giving it.
7. Sell yourself first if you want to sell anything.
8. Be careful reading health books. You may die of a misprint.
9. The best way to find out if you can trust somebody is to trust them.
10. The sure way to lose happiness found, is to want   it at the expense of everything else.
11. Life is a lot like jazz: it's best when you improvise.

12. There's nothing like a cross country bus trip to make you never again want to take a cross country bus trip.

13. Long ago when men jumped up and down, cursed, waved their arms in the air and beat the ground with sticks, it was called witchcraft. Today it is called golf.

14. He who laughs last didn't get it.

15. Once in his life every man is entitled to fall madly in love with a gorgeous red head.

16. It is really depressing to see toys I used to play with being sold as antiques.

17. The longest word that can be spelled without repeating a letter is "uncopyrightable".

18. Why did God make man before he made woman? Because he didn't want any advice on how to do it.

19. A stumble may prevent a fall.

20. Middle age is when a man thinks that in a week or two, he will feel as good as ever.

21. If you are going through Hell, keep going.

22. Joyce and I have the best pre-nuptial agreement in the world. It's called love.

23. The times are not so bad as they seem, they couldn't be.

24. Resentment is like taking poison and waiting for the other person to die.

25. My doctor asked me if I ever had a stress test. I said sure, every day.

26. It isn't true about the watched pot: it boils at the exact same rate as the pot that isn't being watched.
27. The only sure thing about luck is that it will change.
28. Fast food restaurants should have three windows: where you pay, where you pick up and where they fix your order.
29. Half the world is composed of people who have something to say and can't, and the other half who have nothing to say and keep on saying it.
30. A conference is a gathering of people who singly can do nothing – but together can decide that nothing can be done.
31. The man who has eaten enough will never believe a hungry one.
32. No matter how much cats fight, there always seems to be plenty of kittens,
33. It is difficult to think anything but pleasant thoughts while eating a home-grown tomato.
34. Pearls will dissolve in vinegar over time.
35. There is far too much law for those who can afford it, and far too little for those who cannot.
36. Stop letting people who do so little for you control so much of your mind, feelings and emotions.
37. When do the side effects outweigh the benefits?
38. Happiness is not the absence of problems but the ability to deal with them.

39. If I had a nickel for every time I didn't have a nickel, I'd have a lot of nickels.
40. Behold the turtle. He makes progress only when he sticks his neck out!
41. It was not until quite late in life that I discovered how easy it is to say, "I don't know".
42. The best way to cheer yourself is to try to cheer someone else.
43. I find that even when I am sick and depressed, I love life.
44. The best helping hand you will ever receive is the one at the end of you own arm.
45. Life is like a game of chess, changing with each move.
46. It's the friends you can call at 4 am that matter.
47. If you can see things out of whack, then you can see how things can be in whack.
48. All that glitters is not gold, but if there is chocolate inside the foil, who cares?
49. It takes the longest time to understand nothing.
50. A jury consists of 12 people chosen to decide who has the best lawyer.
51. Beware of monotony; it is the mother of all deadly sins.
52. There is no psychiatry like a puppy licking your face.
53. A clear conscious is a result of a poor memory.
54. Months that begin on Sunday will have a Friday the 13th.

55. Doing business without advertising is like winking at a girl in the dark: you know what you are doing but nobody else does.
56. Quarrels would not last as long if the fault was only on one side.
57. As much as pet care costs these days, we should be able to claim our pets as dependents.
58. The wonder of a single snowflake outweighs the wisdom of a million meteorologists.
59. Heroes don't wear capes, they wear dog tags.
60. Just be yourself, it is the only way it can work.
61. Death is nothing to fear, but it is something to prepare for.
62. Now days people know the price of everything and the value of nothing,
63. There are no clocks in Las Vegas gambling casinos.
64. I have one doctor whose only job is to keep track of all my other doctors.
65. Don't tell me not to burn the candle at both ends. Tell me where to get more wax.
66. It doesn't matter how many coins you throw in a fountain, your wishes won't come true.
67. Marriage can be like a deck of cards. In the beginning all you need is two hearts and a diamond. By the end you wish you had a club and a spade.
68. Many people are afraid to say what they want. That's why they don't get what they want.

69. We can't go back to yesterday because we were different people then,

70. Anyone who thinks the air is free has never bought a bag of potato chips.

71. Yesterday is history. Tomorrow is a mystery, today is God's gift. That is why we call it the present.

72. I bought some five-hour energy drinks the past year, but they turned out to be too exhausting.

73. One of the unfortunate things about this world is that good habits are much easier to give up than bad ones.

74. The sum of all the numbers on a roulette wheel is 666.

75. Bifocals are God's way of saying "Keep your chin up".

76. You can never be late for anything in London. They have a huge clock right in the middle of town.

77. You must be going to a pretty awful place if getting there is half the fun.

78. Whenever you are having a bad day, think of the guy who has to put the circus tent back in the bag,

79. Why do dogs always race to the door when the doorbell rings? It's hardly ever for them.

80. Never forget that professionals built the Titanic and amateurs built the Ark.

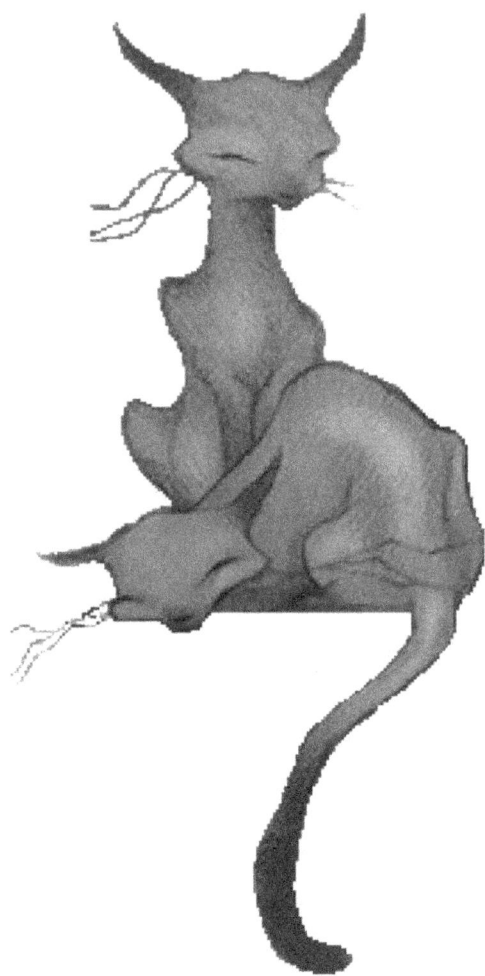

Other titles by Diana Hannon Forrester

Glory
Where have all the Flowers Gone?
All the World's a Stage

With Jan Biggs and Mary Clark
Writing as Alma Lynn Thompson

The Guild in the Granary
Timeless Star
Double Wedding Ring

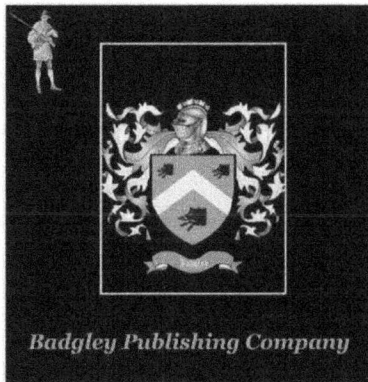

Badgley Publishing Company

For more great stories please visit our website:

www.BadgleyPublishingCompany.com

www.ingramcontent.com/pod-product-compliance
Lightning Source LLC
Chambersburg PA
CBHW031559040426

42452CB00006B/352